basix

Mozart

Guitar TAB Classics

T0004416

12 well-known pieces by one of the world's greatest composers, arranged for guitar

ONLINE ACCESS INCLUDED

Stream or download the audio content for this book.
To access, visit: **alfred.com/redeem**
Enter the following code: 00-22633_449944

Alfred

alfred.com

ISBN-10: 0-7390-3405-7
ISBN-13: 978-0-7390-3405-7

Audio recorded by Howard Wallach at Erich Avinger Studios, Houston, TX

Table of Contents

Wolfgang Amadeus Mozart 3

Signs, Symbols and Terms 4

Minuet in C 5

Allegro in D 6

Andante in E 8

Minuet, K. 94 9

Eine Kleine Nachtmusik, K. 325
    Movement I, Allegro (Themes) 10
    Movement II, Romanze 14
    Movement III, Rondo (Themes) 16

Minuet from *Don Giovanni* 20

Sonata in C, K. 545
    Movement I (Themes) 21

Andante, K. 487 24

Allegro, K. 487 28

Adagio, K. 356 31

Rondo Alla Turca, K. 331 36

A Musical Joke, K. 522
    Movement IV 41

Track 1 There is a recording included with this book. It includes performances of all the pieces. Use it to help insure that you are interpreting the rhythms correctly and capturing the style of each work. This symbol will appear to the left of each piece. The track numbers correspond to the piece you want to hear. Track 1 will help you tune to the recording. Enjoy!

Wolfgang Amadeus Mozart

Wolfgang Amadeus Mozart was born in Salzburg, Austria, on January 27, 1756. His first efforts at composition began when he was only four years old. By the time he was six he had composed dozens of remarkable pieces for the keyboard as well as for other instruments, and was performing for emperors and empresses in the courts of Europe.

At eight, he startled the King of England by playing at sight every difficult piece of music put before him, and by improvising during public concerts. At the age of 10, he wrote an oratorio, and at 11, he wrote his first opera. At 13 he was appointed Chapel Master at the court of the Archbishop of Salzburg. At 14, he received an advanced degree in music from the Royal Academy in Mantua, Italy, and was knighted by the Pope. By this time, he had successful operas running for weeks of performance at La Scala, the great opera house in Milan, Italy, and was no longer regarded as a child prodigy, but fully recognized as a great master.

Wolfgang's father, Leopold Mozart, was a famous violinist who held an important position as the assistant conductor of the orchestra of the Archbishop of Salzburg. He was a brilliant musician and an outstanding teacher, and he was quick to recognize the unusual talents of his two remarkable children. Wolfgang's sister, Anna Maria (Nannerl), was almost as gifted as her brother. Leopold virtually gave up his post with the court orchestra to devote his time to developing the talents of his two children, and to arranging concert appearances for them.

During his extensive travels, the young Wolfgang was quick to assimilate the best of what he heard from the greatest musicians he encountered. In London, he studied composition with Johann Christian Bach, a son of the great Johann Sebastian Bach. In Germany, he was impressed and influenced by the musical discipline of the famous Mannheim Orchestra, with its remarkable dynamic contrasts, ranging from the softest pianissimo to the loudest fortissimo. In Bologna, Italy, he was heard by the great Padre Martini, who became his mentor and instructor and helped him to prepare for his degree.

When he was 26 years old, Mozart married Constanze von Weber, over his father's objections. The course of his married life never ran smooth. Although his career was artistically successful, he was a poor business man and had a difficult time managing his affairs, especially after his father was no longer able to travel with him. Although his music was performed all over Europe, even by amateurs and (to Mozart's delight) by street musicians, Mozart died in poor circumstances. Believing that he had been poisoned, perhaps by a jealous musician, he died on December 5, 1791, and was buried in an unmarked grave.

Mozart's works contain the essence as well as the most perfect of those compositions which are correctly called classical. His fame came first as a composer and performer of music for the harpsichord, but the piano began to be perfected, and by the time he was 21, he had selected it for his main instrument. He became the first of the great composers for piano.

Of Wolfgang Amadeus Mozart, Haydn said, "He is the greatest composer I know, personally or by reputation. He has taste, and furthermore he has the greatest possible knowledge of composition."

Mozart would never bow to the common practice of allowing royalty to dictate how music should be composed. When the Emperor heard his opera The Abduction from the Seraglio, he said, "It is too beautiful, my dear Mozart, and it has far too many notes." Wolfgang answered, quite confidently, "Just exactly as many notes as are needed, Your Majesty."

Signs, Symbols and Terms

Roman Numerals

I	1	IV	4	VII	7	X	10
II	2	V	5	VIII	8	XI	11
III	3	VI	6	IX	9	XII	12

adagio = A slow tempo which is faster than *largo* and slower than *andante*.

allegro = Cheerful, quick or fast.

allegretto = A lively quick tempo that moves more slowly than *allegro*.

andante = A moderate, graceful tempo, slower than *allegretto* and faster than *adagio*.

a tempo = Return to the original tempo.

cantabile = Singing.

commodo = Comfortable, leisurely.

con brio = With vigor.

con moto = With motion.

cresc. = Abbreviation for *crescendo*. Gradually becoming louder. ◁

D.C. al Fine = *Da capo al fine*. Go back to the beginning of the piece and play to the *Fine*, which is the end of the piece.

dim. = Abbreviation for *diminuendo*. Gradually becoming softer. ▷

dolce = Sweet.

gliss. = Abbreviation for *glissando*. To slide from one note to another. Often shown as a diagonal line with an S (slide) in guitar music.

harm. = Abbreviation for *harmonic*. Notes of the harmonic series that are very pure and clear. In this book, written at the sounding pitch with a diamond shaped note head. Touch the string lightly directly over the indicated fret and pluck, immediately removing the finger from the string.

largo = Very slow and broad.

legato = Smooth, connected.

leggiero = Light or delicate.

BV₃ = **Barre three strings at the 5th fret.**

BV = **Barre all six strings at the 5th fret.**

HBV = **Hinge barre at the 5th fret. Play an individual note on the 1st string with the bottom of the 1st finger, just above the palm. Usually simplifies the next fingering.**

⑥ = D = **Tune the 6th string down to D**

p, i, m, a = **The right-hand fingers starting with the thumb.**

1, 2, 3, 4, 0 = **The left-hand fingers starting with the index finger, and the open string.**

> = *Accent.* **Emphasize the note.**

〰 = *Arpeggiate.* **Quickly "roll" the chord.**

⋀ = *Marcato.* **Emphasize more than an accent.**

l.v. = Abbreviation for *laissez vibre* (let vibrate).

maestoso = Sublime or magnificent.

moderato = In a moderate tempo.

molto = Very or much.

non troppo = But not too much so.

più = More.

poco a poco = Little by little.

rall. = Abbreviation for *rallentando*. Becoming gradually slower.

rit. = Abbreviation for *ritardando*. Becoming gradually slower.

sempre = Always.

sostenuto = Sustained.

staccato = Short, detached. ♪ ♩

tranquillo = Tranquil, calm, quiet.

vivace = Lively, quick.

Reading Tablature

Tablature is a purely graphic way of showing what to play on the guitar. There are six lines, each representing one of the strings. Numbers placed on the lines indicate what fret to play on that string.

In this book, the tablature is always written parallel to the standard notation, which already contains all the rhythmic information, so the tablature only indicates the fret numbers and strings.

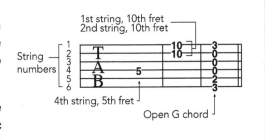

Minuet in C

 Track 2

⌅ = *Mordent.* Quickly hammer-on to the *upper neighbor* (C) and then pull-off to the B.

Allegro in D

 Track 3

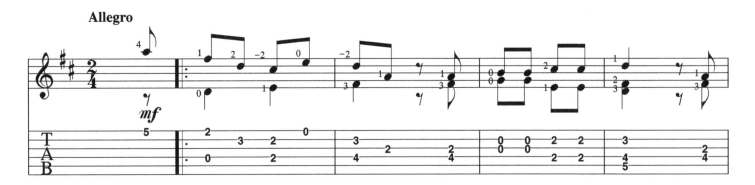

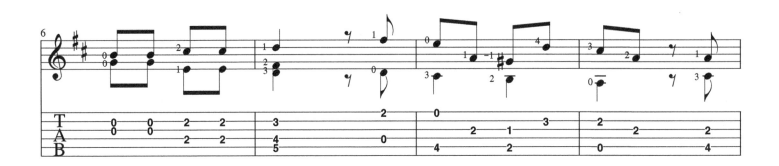

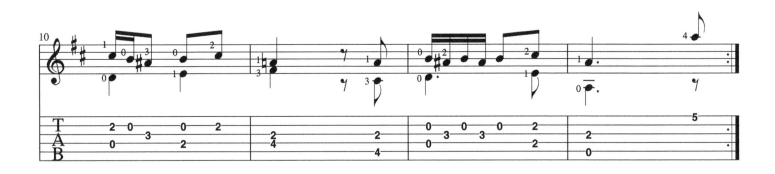

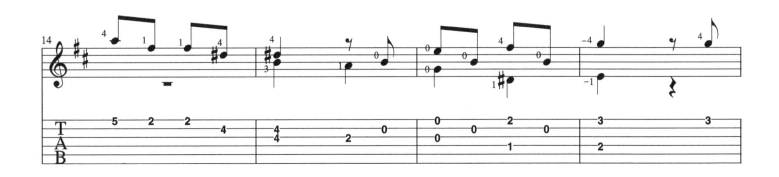

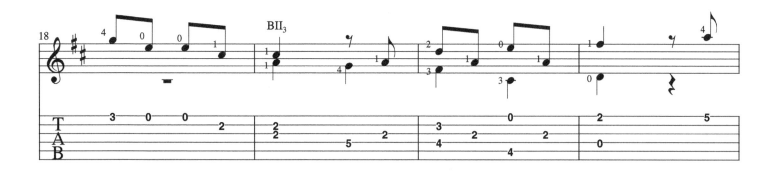

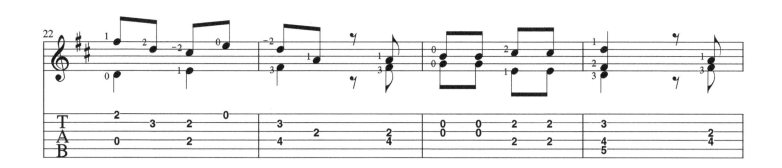

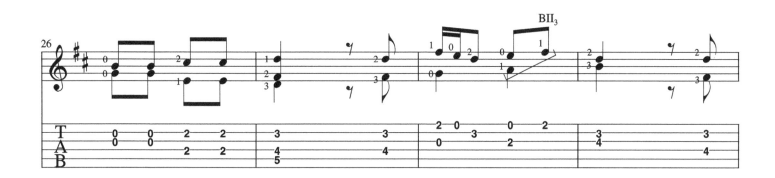

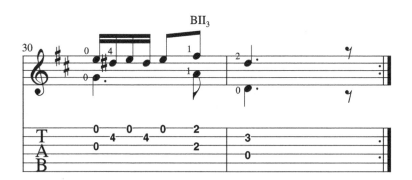

Andante in E

 Track 4

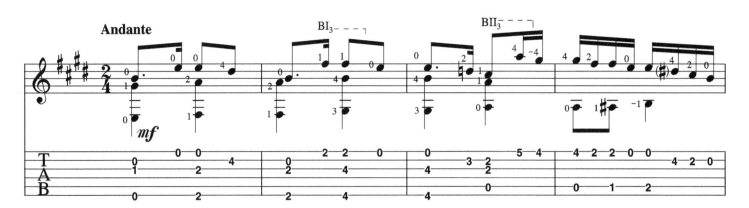

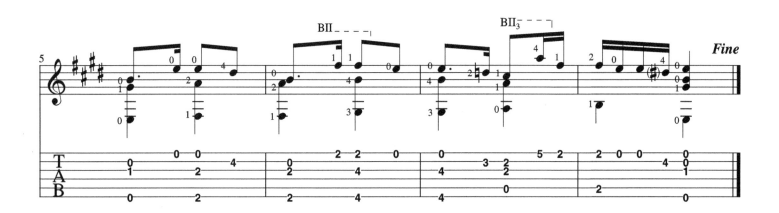

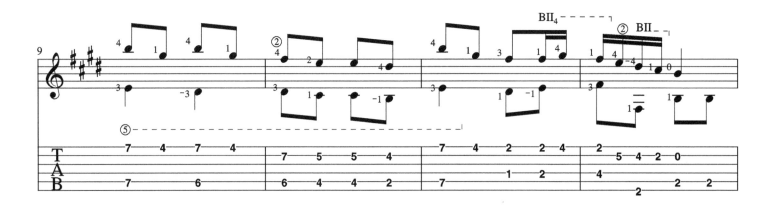

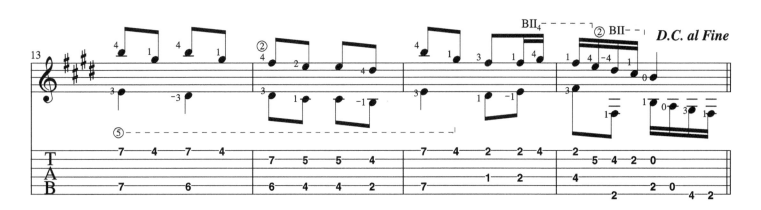

Minuet, K.94

 Track 5

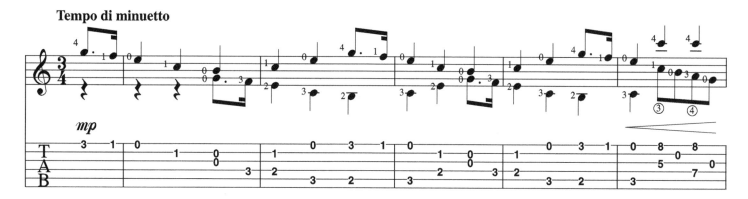

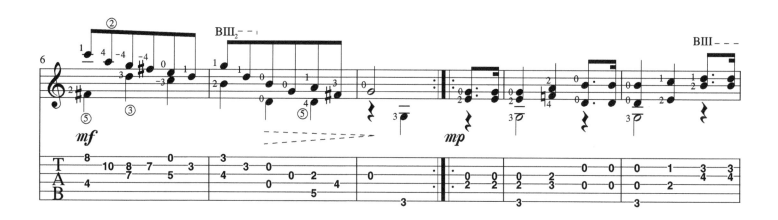

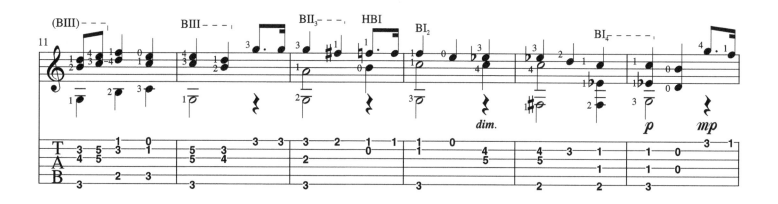

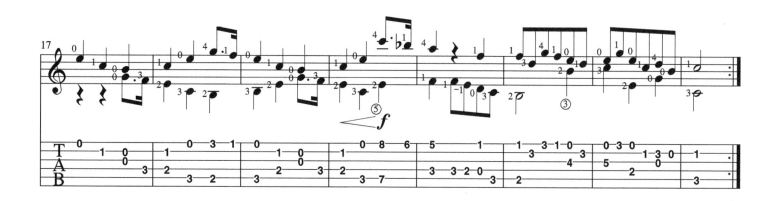

Eine Kleine Nacht Musik, K. 325

Movement I, Allegro (Themes)

 Track 6

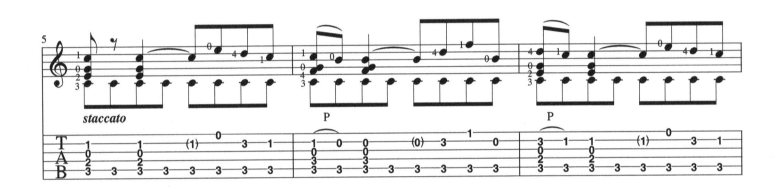

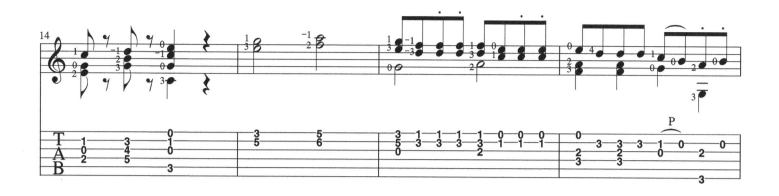

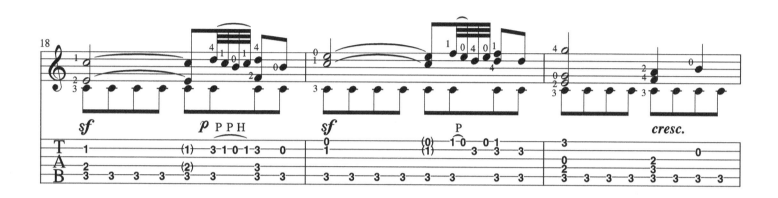

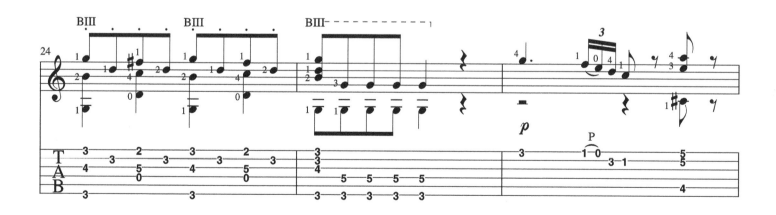

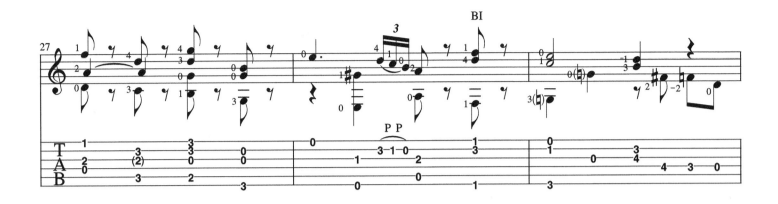

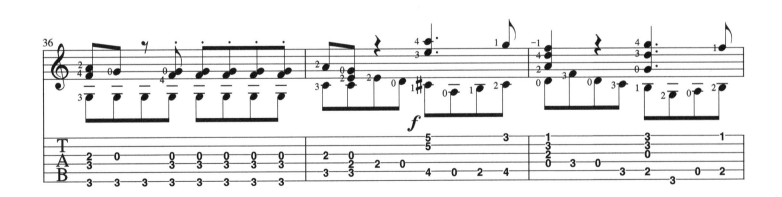

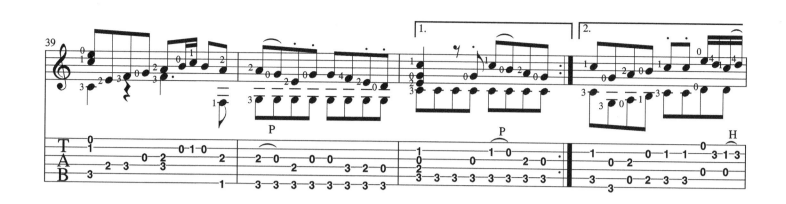

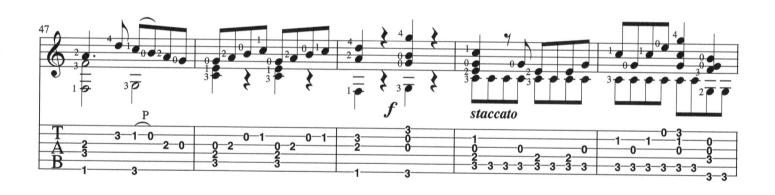

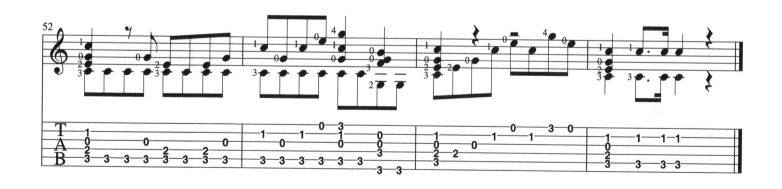

Movement II, Romanze

 Track 7

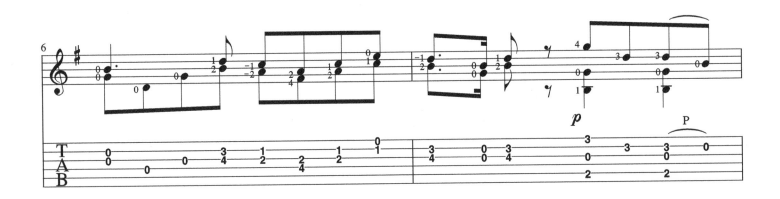

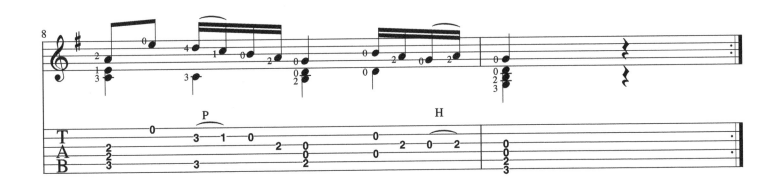

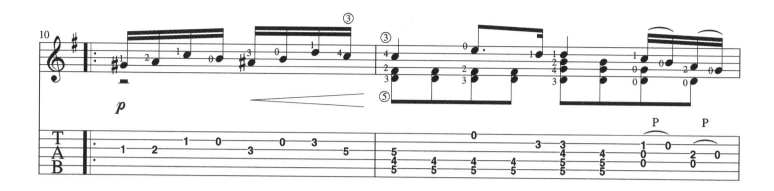

16

Movement III, Rondo

(Themes)

Track 8

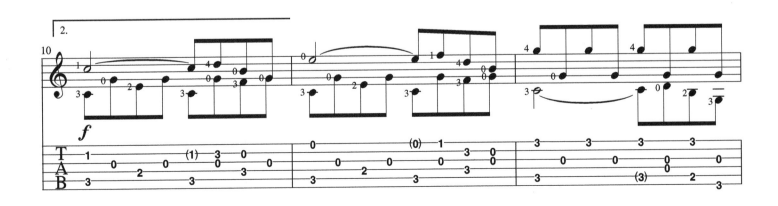

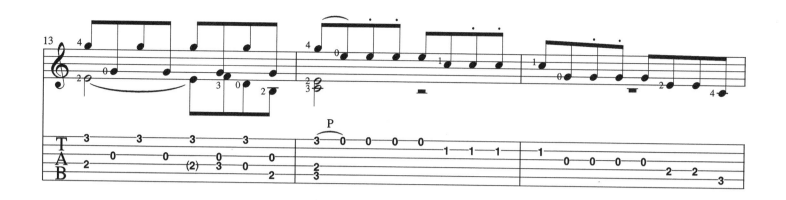

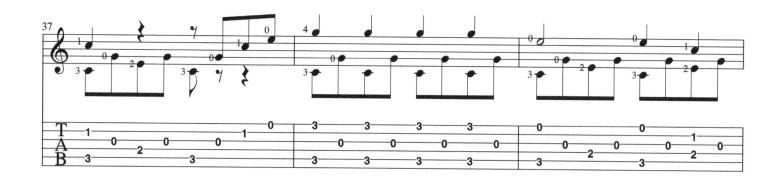

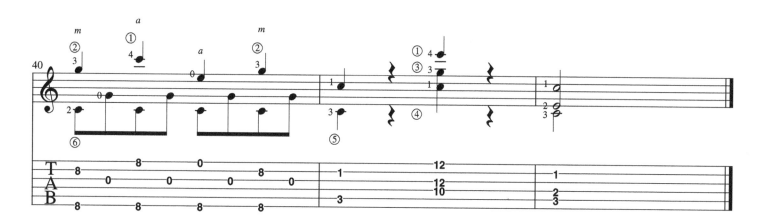

Minuet

from *Don Giovanni*

 Track 9

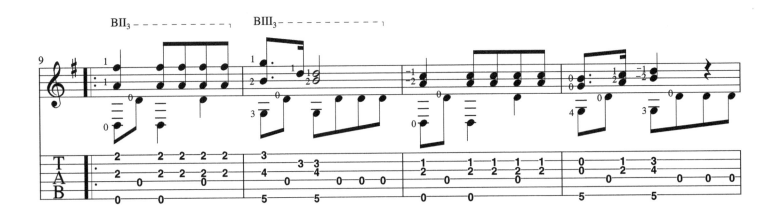

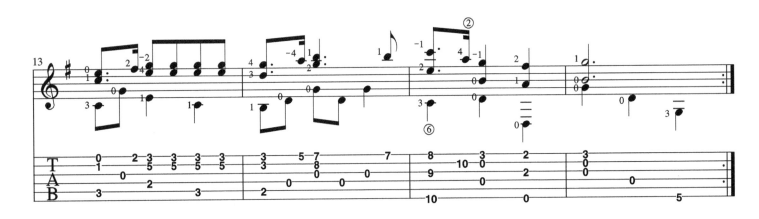

Sonata in C, K. 545

Movement I (Themes)

 Track 10

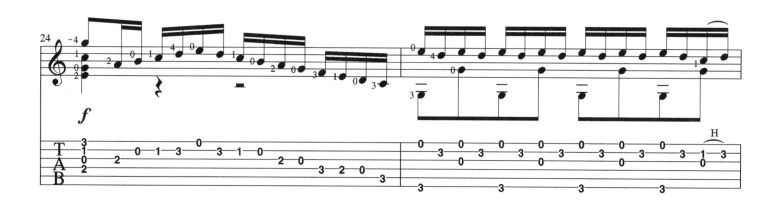

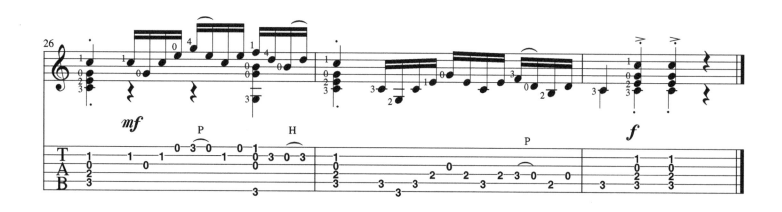

Andante, K. 487

Track 11

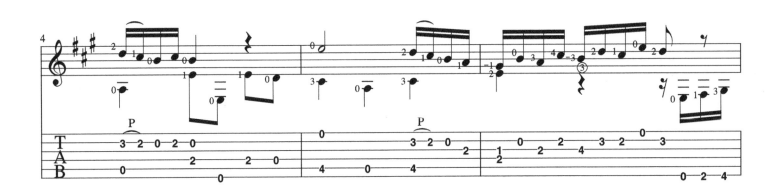

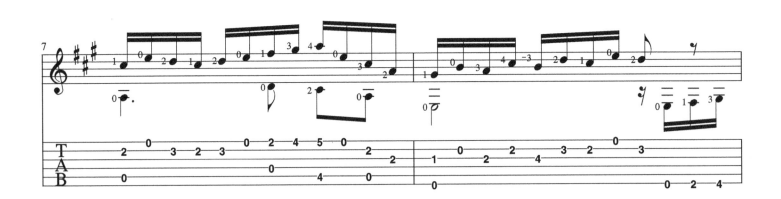

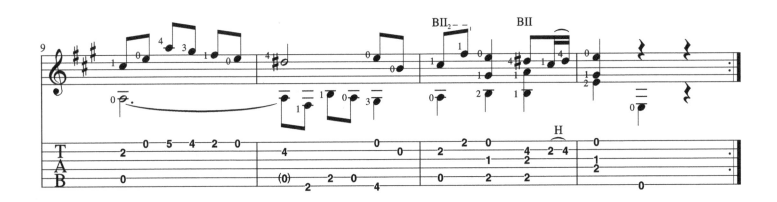

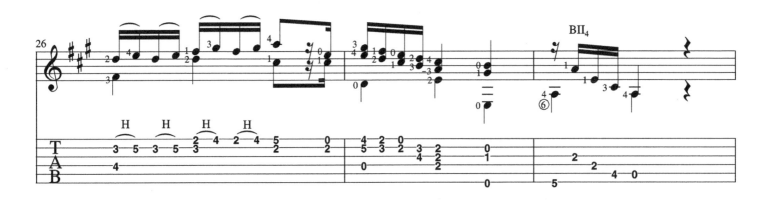

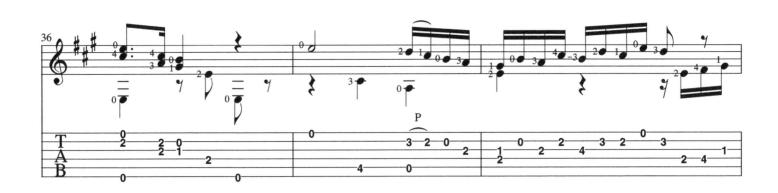

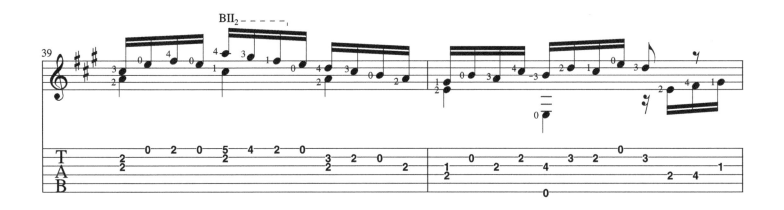

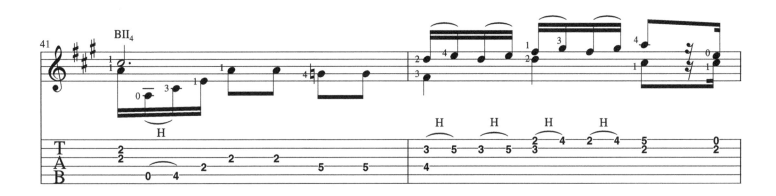

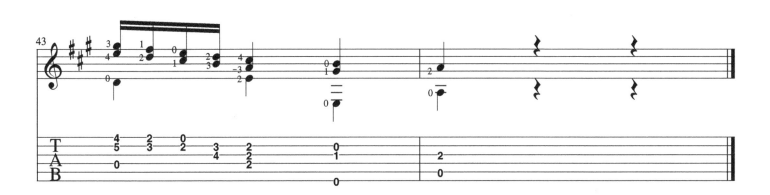

Allegro, K. 487

Track 12

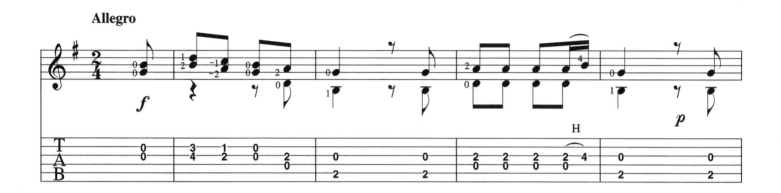

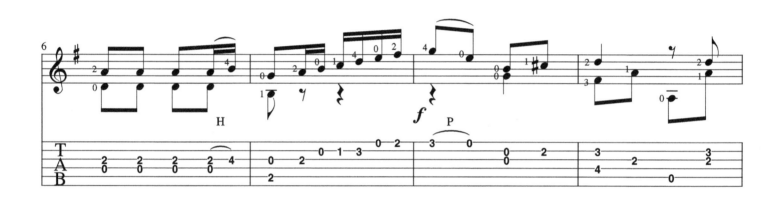

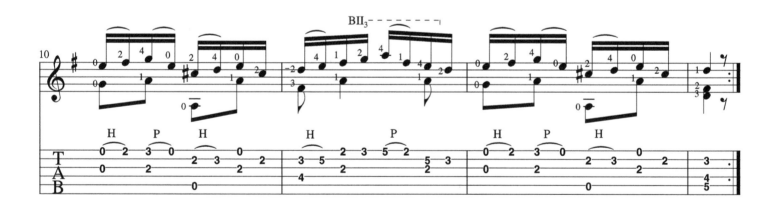

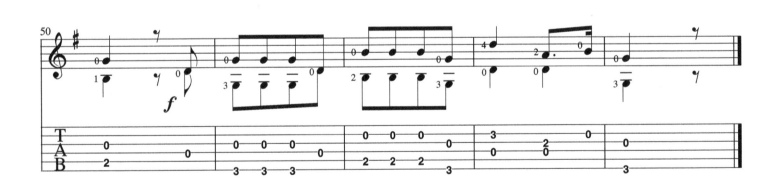

Adagio, K. 356

 Track 13

Adagio

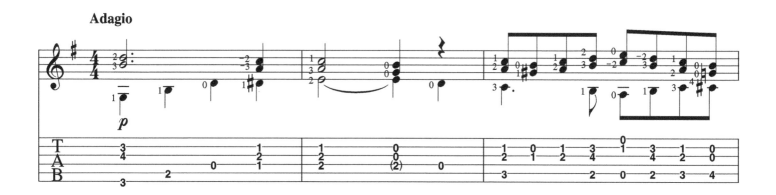

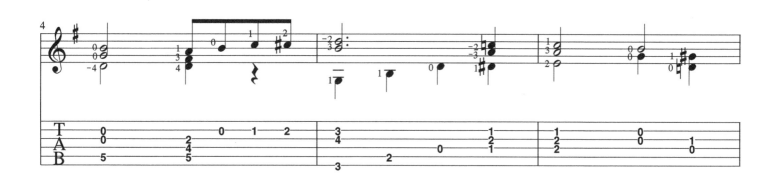

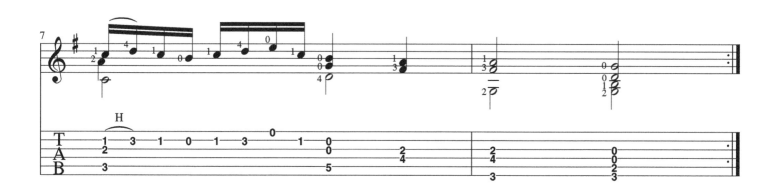

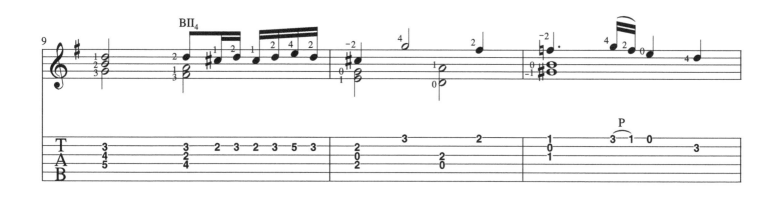

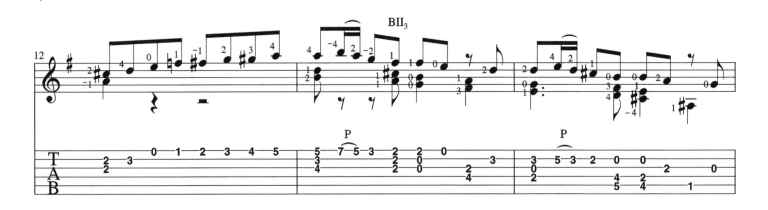

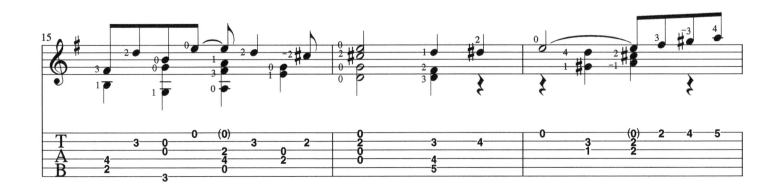

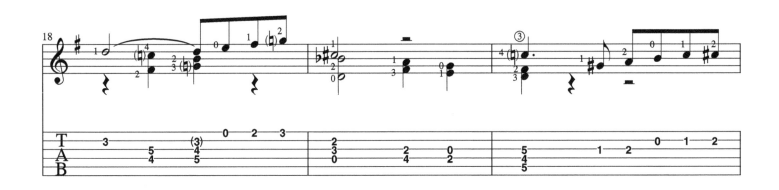

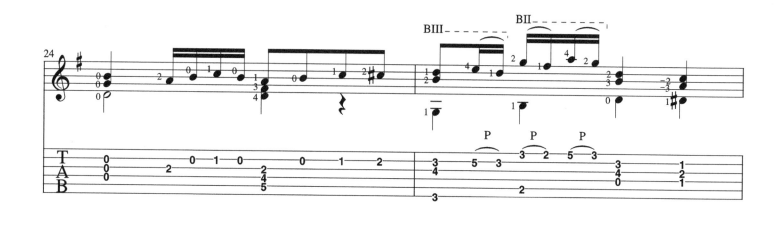

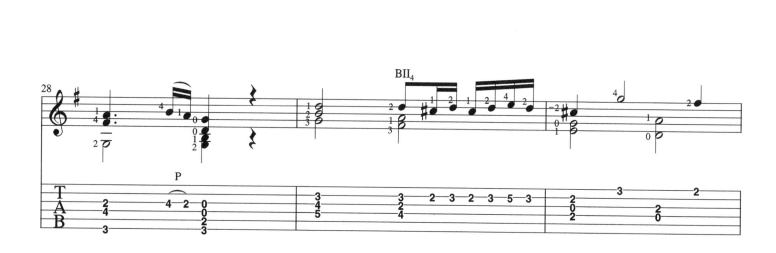

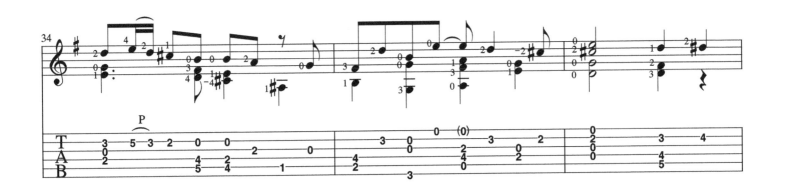

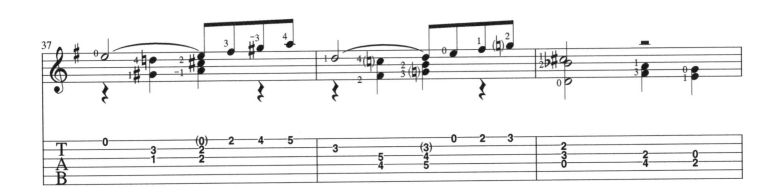

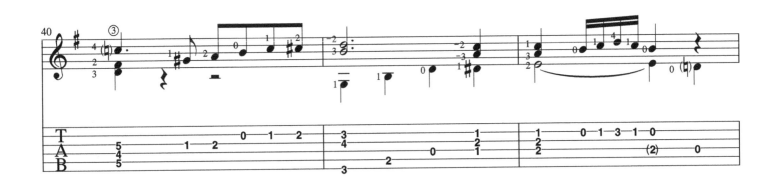

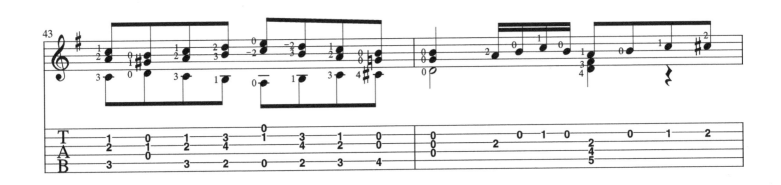

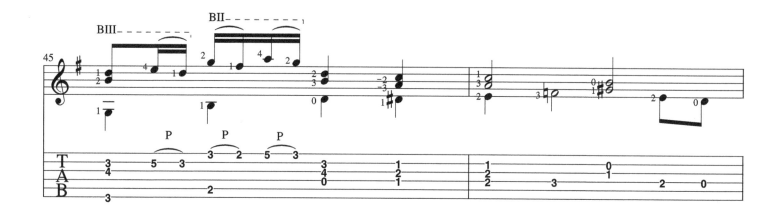

Rondo Alla Turca, K. 331

 Track 14

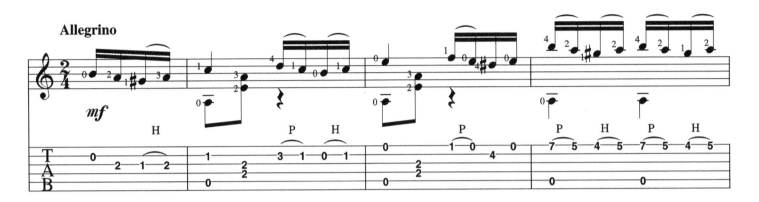

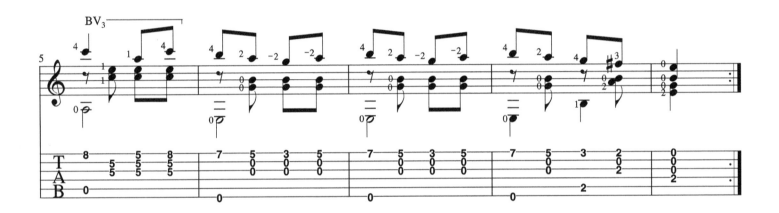

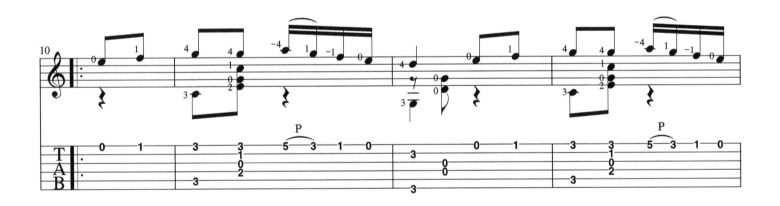

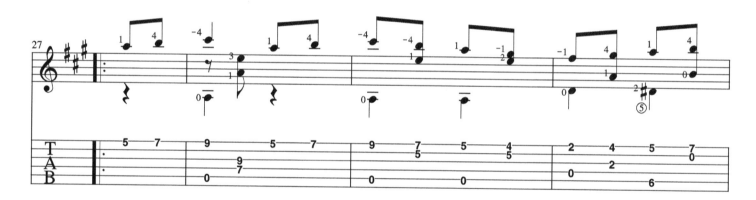

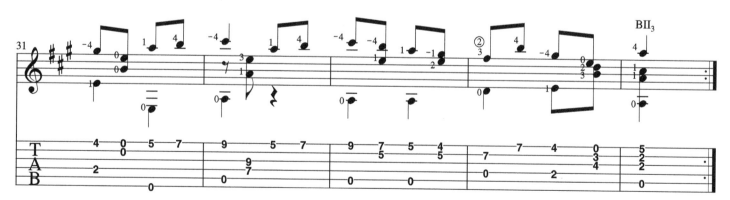

* **tr** = **Trill.** Start on the upper neighbor (C) and quickly pull-off/hammer-on several times, ending on the B.

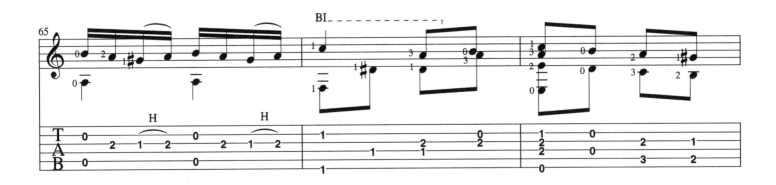

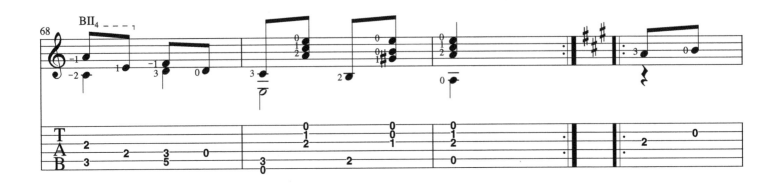

D.C. al Fine

A Musical Joke, K. 522

Movement IV

Track 15

Allegro vivace

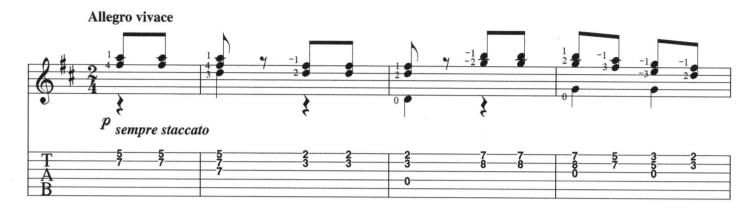

p sempre staccato

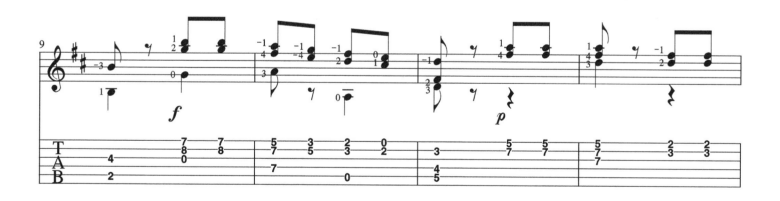

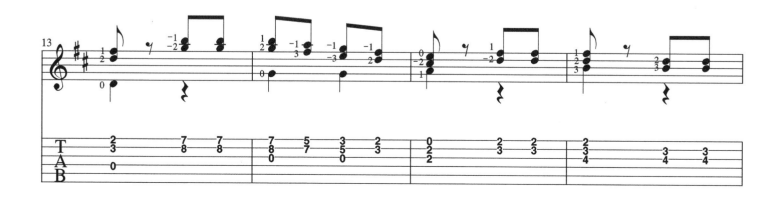

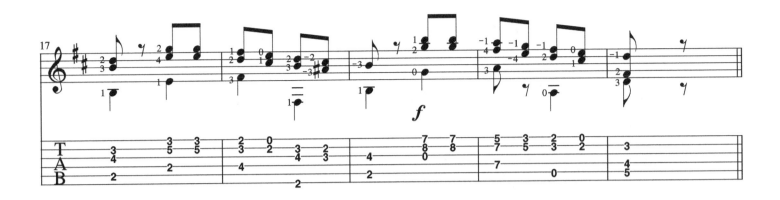

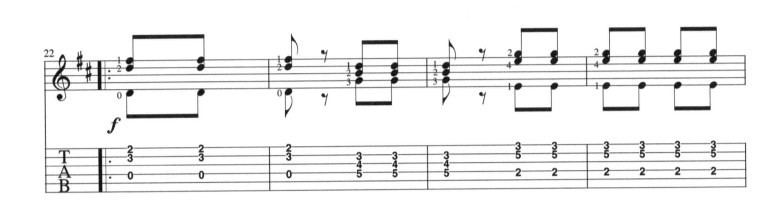

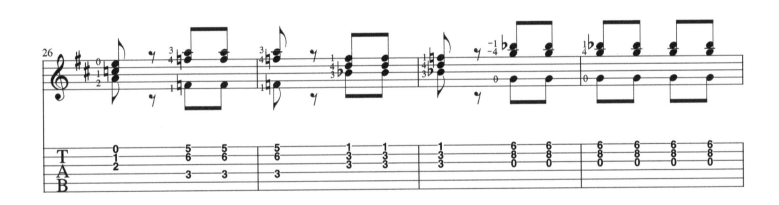

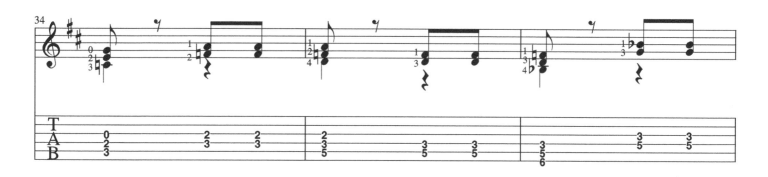

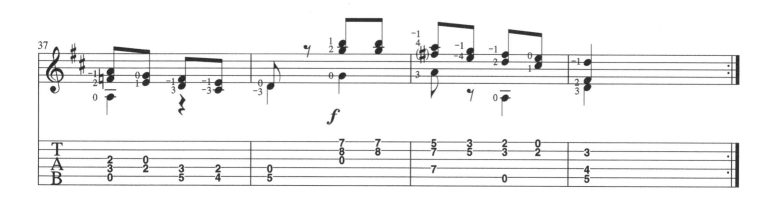